Chapter 1: Introduction to Health and Safety for Small Businesses in the UK

Chapter 2: Health and Safety Regulations for Retail Businesses in the UK

Chapter 3: Health and Safety Guidelines for Small Medical Practices in the UK

Chapter 4: Workplace Safety Training for Small Construction Businesses in the UK

Chapter 5: Health and Safety Requirements for Food Service Establishments in the UK

Chapter 6: Health and Safety Protocols for Small Manufacturing Businesses in the UK

Chapter 7: Occupational Health and Safety for Small Businesses in the UK

Chapter 8: Health and Safety Compliance for Small Businesses in the Hospitality Industry in the UK

Chapter 9: Mental Health and Well-being Initiatives for Small Businesses in the UK

Chapter 10: Health and Safety Considerations for Small Businesses Operating Remotely in the UK

Chapter 11: First Aid and Emergency Response Planning for Small Businesses in the UK

Conclusion: Ensuring a Safe and Healthy Work Environment for Small Businesses in the UK

01

Chapter 1: Introduction to Health and Safety for Small Businesses in the UK

Understanding the Importance of Health and Safety in the Workplace

In the fast-paced world of small businesses in the UK, the importance of health and safety in the workplace cannot be overstated. As a small business owner or manager, it is crucial to understand the significance of implementing proper health and safety measures to protect your employees, customers, and business as a whole.

One of the key reasons why health and safety in the workplace is essential is to prevent accidents and injuries. By identifying potential hazards and implementing safety protocols, you can reduce the risk of workplace accidents and ensure the well-being of your employees. This not only protects your staff but also helps you avoid costly legal battles and compensation claims that could potentially cripple your business.

Moreover, prioritizing health and safety in the workplace can also improve employee morale and productivity. When your employees feel safe and valued, they are more likely to be motivated and engaged in their work. This can lead to increased productivity, better quality of work, and ultimately, a more successful business.

Additionally, complying with health and safety regulations is a legal requirement for all businesses in the UK. Failure to meet these regulations can result in fines, penalties, and even criminal prosecution. By staying informed about the latest health and safety guidelines and ensuring your workplace is compliant, you can protect your business from legal repercussions and maintain a good reputation within your industry.

Overall, understanding the importance of health and safety in the workplace is crucial for the success and longevity of your small business. Whether you operate in the retail, medical, construction, food service, manufacturing, hospitality, or any other industry, prioritizing health and safety should be a top priority. By investing in proper training, safety protocols, and emergency response planning, you can create a safe and secure work environment for your employees and customers, ultimately setting your business up for long-term success.

Overview of Health and Safety Regulations in the UK

Health and safety regulations are an essential aspect of running a small business in the UK. These regulations are in place to protect the health and well-being of employees, customers, and visitors to your business premises. By understanding and complying with these regulations, you can create a safe and healthy working environment for everyone involved.

For small retail businesses in the UK, health and safety regulations cover a wide range of areas, including fire safety, manual handling, and the safe storage of goods. It is important to conduct regular risk assessments to identify potential hazards in your store and take steps to mitigate them. Training your staff on health and safety procedures is also crucial to ensure everyone knows how to respond in an emergency.

In small medical practices, health and safety guidelines are particularly important due to the nature of the work being carried out. In addition to the standard regulations that apply to all businesses, medical practices must also adhere to specific guidelines related to infection control, waste disposal, and patient confidentiality. Implementing proper hygiene protocols and ensuring staff are trained in emergency procedures are key aspects of maintaining a safe environment for patients and employees.

For small construction businesses in the UK, workplace safety training is essential to prevent accidents and injuries on the job. This includes providing proper training on the use of equipment, ensuring that workers wear appropriate protective gear, and conducting regular safety inspections of the work site. By prioritizing safety in your construction business, you can reduce the risk of accidents and create a more productive and efficient work environment.

In the food service industry, health and safety requirements in the UK are particularly stringent to protect against foodborne illnesses and ensure the safety of customers. This includes proper food handling and storage practices, regular cleaning and sanitation of kitchen equipment, and training staff on food safety procedures. By following these regulations, you can maintain a high standard of hygiene in your establishment and protect the health of your customers.

Common Health and Safety Hazards in Small Businesses

Small businesses in the UK face a variety of health and safety hazards that can impact the well-being of employees and the success of the business. It is crucial for small business owners and managers to be aware of these hazards and take steps to mitigate risks in order to create a safe and healthy work environment for their employees.

One common health and safety hazard in small businesses is slips, trips, and falls. These accidents can occur due to wet or uneven floors, cluttered workspaces, or inadequate lighting. To prevent slips, trips, and falls, small business owners should ensure that floors are kept clean and dry, walkways are clear of obstacles, and proper lighting is in place. Additionally, employees should be trained on safe work practices and encouraged to report any hazards they encounter. Another common hazard in small businesses is manual handling injuries. This can occur when employees lift, carry, or move heavy objects without proper training or equipment. Small business owners should provide training on safe lifting techniques, as well as access to mechanical aids such as trolleys or lifting equipment. It is also important to assess the risks associated with manual handling tasks and make adjustments to reduce the likelihood of injury.

Exposure to hazardous substances is another health and safety hazard that small businesses need to be aware of. This can include chemicals, fumes, or dust that can cause respiratory problems, skin irritation, or other health issues. Small business owners should conduct risk assessments to identify potential hazards, provide appropriate Personal Protective Equipment (PPE) to employees, and implement controls to minimize exposure to hazardous substances.

Fire safety is a crucial consideration for small businesses, as fires can have devastating consequences for both employees and the business itself. Small business owners should ensure that fire exits are clearly marked and unobstructed, fire alarms are regularly tested, and employees are trained on evacuation procedures. It is also important to have fire extinguishers and other firefighting equipment readily available and regularly maintained.

In conclusion, small business owners and managers in the UK must be proactive in identifying and addressing health and safety hazards in their workplaces. By taking steps to prevent slips, trips, and falls, manual handling injuries, exposure to hazardous substances, and fire hazards, small businesses can create a safer and healthier work environment for their employees. This not only protects the well-being of employees but also ensures the long-term success and sustainability of the business.

02

Chapter 2: Health and Safety Regulations for Retail Businesses in the UK

Specific Regulations for Retail Businesses

When it comes to health and safety regulations for retail businesses in the UK, there are several key guidelines that small business owners and managers need to be aware of. Firstly, it is important to ensure that your premises are safe for both employees and customers. This includes regular risk assessments to identify any potential hazards, such as trip hazards, faulty equipment, or poor lighting. By addressing these issues promptly, you can help prevent accidents and injuries in your store.

In addition to maintaining a safe physical environment, retail businesses in the UK must also comply with regulations regarding the handling and storage of goods. This includes ensuring that items are stored safely and securely to prevent accidents such as falling objects or slips and trips. It is also important to provide adequate training for employees on how to safely handle merchandise, especially if they are working with heavy or hazardous materials.

Another important regulation for retail businesses in the UK is fire safety. It is essential to have a comprehensive fire safety plan in place, including regular fire drills and training for staff on how to respond in the event of a fire. This should also include having appropriate fire detection and suppression systems installed, as well as clearly marked evacuation routes and assembly points.

In addition to physical safety measures, retail businesses in the UK must also consider the mental health and well-being of their employees. This includes providing a supportive work environment, promoting work-life balance, and offering mental health resources and support. By prioritizing the mental health of your team, you can help reduce stress and improve overall productivity in your store.

Overall, by following these specific regulations for retail businesses in the UK, small business owners and managers can create a safe and healthy work environment for their employees and customers. By prioritizing health and safety in your store, you can not only comply with legal requirements but also enhance the overall well-being and success of your business.

Safety Guidelines for Customer-Facing Roles

Safety guidelines for customer-facing roles are essential for small businesses in the UK to ensure the well-being of both employees and customers. Customer-facing roles encompass a wide range of industries, including retail, healthcare, construction, food service, manufacturing, hospitality, and more. By following these guidelines, small business owners and managers can create a safe and secure environment for their staff and customers.

First and foremost, it is crucial for employees in customer-facing roles to undergo proper training on health and safety protocols. This training should cover topics such as emergency response procedures, handling hazardous materials, proper lifting techniques, and customer conflict resolution. By equipping employees with the necessary skills and knowledge, businesses can prevent accidents and injuries in the workplace.

In addition to training, small businesses should implement safety measures to protect both employees and customers. This includes providing personal protective equipment (PPE) such as gloves, masks, and safety goggles, as well as installing security cameras and alarm systems to deter potential threats. Regular safety inspections should also be conducted to identify and address any hazards in the workplace.

Furthermore, small businesses should develop clear communication channels for reporting safety concerns or incidents. Employees should feel comfortable speaking up about any potential risks or hazards they encounter while on the job. By fostering a culture of open communication, businesses can address safety issues promptly and prevent future incidents from occurring.

Lastly, small businesses should stay up-to-date on health and safety regulations specific to their industry. This includes understanding the legal requirements for workplace safety, conducting regular risk assessments, and implementing measures to comply with industry standards. By staying informed and proactive, small businesses can ensure the health and well-being of everyone in the workplace.

Implementing Health and Safety Policies in Retail Environments

Implementing health and safety policies in retail environments is crucial for small business owners and managers in the UK. By creating and enforcing these policies, businesses can ensure the well-being of their employees and customers, as well as comply with health and safety regulations. This subchapter will provide guidance on how to effectively implement health and safety policies in retail settings.

One of the first steps in implementing health and safety policies in a retail environment is to conduct a thorough risk assessment. This involves identifying potential hazards in the workplace, such as slippery floors, heavy lifting, or exposure to harmful chemicals. By understanding these risks, businesses can take appropriate measures to mitigate them and create a safer work environment for everyone.

Once risks have been identified, it is important to develop and communicate clear health and safety policies to all employees. This includes outlining procedures for reporting accidents or incidents, as well as providing training on how to handle emergencies. By ensuring that everyone is aware of the policies and procedures in place, businesses can help prevent accidents and injuries from occurring.

In addition to implementing policies, businesses should regularly review and update their health and safety practices to ensure they remain effective. This may involve conducting regular inspections of the workplace, providing ongoing training to employees, and staying informed about any changes to health and safety regulations. By staying proactive and responsive to potential risks, businesses can create a culture of safety within their retail environment.

Overall, implementing health and safety policies in retail environments is essential for small business owners and managers in the UK. By taking proactive steps to identify and mitigate risks, communicate policies effectively, and stay informed about regulations, businesses can create a safe and healthy workplace for their employees and customers. By prioritizing health and safety, businesses can not only protect their workforce, but also enhance their reputation and ensure long-term success.

03

Chapter 3: Health and Safety Guidelines for Small Medical Practices in the UK

Compliance with Health and Safety Regulations in Medical Settings

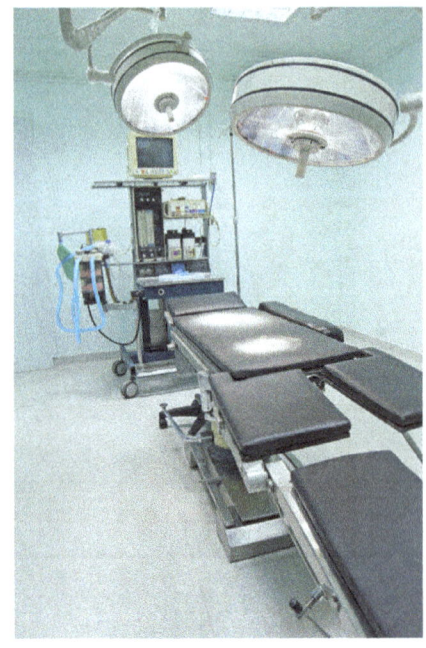

Compliance with health and safety regulations is crucial in all workplaces, but it is particularly important in medical settings where the well-being of patients and staff is at stake. Small business owners and managers in UK medical practices must ensure that they are following all relevant health and safety guidelines to protect their employees and patients.

One of the key aspects of compliance with health and safety regulations in medical settings is ensuring that all staff are properly trained in handling hazardous materials and waste. This includes proper disposal of medical waste, such as sharps and biohazardous materials, as well as using personal protective equipment (PPE) when necessary. By providing thorough training and enforcing strict protocols, small medical practices can reduce the risk of accidents and exposure to harmful substances.

In addition to training on hazardous materials, small medical practices must also have protocols in place for preventing the spread of infectious diseases. This includes regular sanitation of surfaces, proper hand hygiene practices, and protocols for isolating patients with contagious illnesses. By following these guidelines, medical practices can minimize the risk of spreading infections among patients and staff.

Another important aspect of compliance with health and safety regulations in medical settings is ensuring that all equipment is properly maintained and serviced. This includes regular inspections of medical devices, such as x-ray machines and sterilization equipment, to ensure they are functioning correctly and pose no risk to staff or patients. By staying on top of equipment maintenance, small medical practices can prevent accidents and ensure the safety of everyone in the workplace.

Overall, compliance with health and safety regulations in medical settings is essential for protecting the well-being of employees and patients. Small business owners and managers in UK medical practices must prioritize training, proper sanitation practices, and equipment maintenance to ensure a safe and healthy work environment. By following these guidelines, small medical practices can not only comply with regulations but also create a culture of safety that benefits everyone in the workplace.

Infection Control Measures for Medical Practices

Infection control measures are crucial for medical practices to ensure the safety of both patients and staff. Small business owners and managers in UK businesses operating in the healthcare sector must prioritize implementing effective protocols to prevent the spread of infections within their facilities. By adhering to strict guidelines and best practices, medical practices can reduce the risk of healthcare-associated infections and maintain a safe environment for all stakeholders.

One of the key infection control measures for medical practices is proper hand hygiene. Staff members should be trained on the correct handwashing techniques and encouraged to regularly wash their hands with soap and water or use hand sanitizers. Hand hygiene is essential in preventing the transmission of bacteria and viruses, particularly in healthcare settings where patients may be more susceptible to infections.

In addition to hand hygiene, medical practices should also implement protocols for cleaning and disinfecting surfaces and equipment. Regular cleaning of high-touch surfaces such as doorknobs, countertops, and medical equipment can help prevent the spread of infections. Using appropriate disinfectants and following manufacturer guidelines for cleaning can ensure that pathogens are effectively eliminated from the environment.

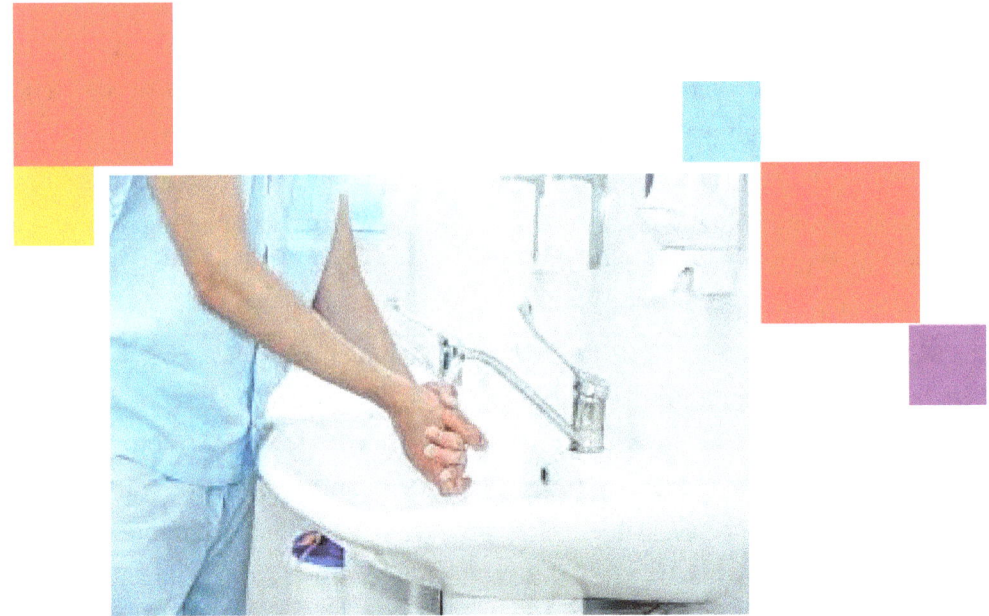

Furthermore, medical practices should establish protocols for the proper handling and disposal of medical waste. Sharps, contaminated linens, and other hazardous materials should be disposed of in accordance with regulations to prevent the spread of infections. Staff members should receive training on how to handle medical waste safely and ensure that waste disposal practices are consistently followed.

Overall, infection control measures are a critical component of maintaining a safe and healthy environment in medical practices. Small business owners and managers in the healthcare industry must prioritize implementing these measures to protect the well-being of their patients and staff. By following best practices for hand hygiene, cleaning and disinfection, and medical waste management, medical practices can minimize the risk of infections and promote a culture of safety within their facilities.

Staff Training for Health and Safety in Medical Environments

In the fast-paced and high-pressure environment of medical practices, ensuring the health and safety of staff is paramount. Staff training plays a crucial role in maintaining a safe workplace for employees in the medical field. From handling hazardous materials to preventing workplace injuries, proper training is essential for small business owners and managers in the UK to comply with health and safety regulations.

One of the key aspects of staff training for health and safety in medical environments is educating employees on the proper procedures for handling hazardous materials. This includes training on how to safely dispose of medical waste, handle potentially infectious materials, and use protective equipment such as gloves and masks. Small business owners and managers in the UK must ensure that all staff members are well-versed in these protocols to prevent accidents and exposure to harmful substances.

In addition to handling hazardous materials, staff training for health and safety in medical environments should also cover proper lifting techniques to prevent workplace injuries. Medical staff often need to lift and move patients, equipment, and supplies, which can put strain on their bodies if not done correctly. Training on proper lifting techniques can help reduce the risk of musculoskeletal injuries and keep employees healthy and safe on the job.

Furthermore, small business owners and managers in the UK should provide staff training on infection control practices to prevent the spread of diseases in medical environments. This includes proper hand hygiene, cleaning and disinfection protocols, and the use of personal protective equipment. By ensuring that all staff members are well-trained in infection control practices, medical practices can maintain a clean and safe environment for both employees and patients.

Overall, staff training for health and safety in medical environments is crucial for small business owners and managers in the UK to ensure compliance with regulations and protect the well-being of their employees. By investing in comprehensive training programs that cover handling hazardous materials, proper lifting techniques, and infection control practices, medical practices can create a safe and healthy workplace for their staff. Prioritizing staff training for health and safety not only benefits employees but also contributes to the overall success and reputation of the business.

04

Chapter 4: Workplace Safety Training for Small Construction Businesses in the UK

Health and Safety Requirements for Construction Sites

Health and safety requirements for construction sites are crucial to ensure the well-being of workers and the public. In the UK, small business owners and managers in the construction industry must adhere to strict regulations to prevent accidents and injuries on site. These regulations are in place to protect workers from hazards such as falls, electrical hazards, and exposure to harmful substances.

One key requirement for construction sites is the implementation of a thorough risk assessment. This involves identifying potential hazards on site and taking steps to eliminate or reduce them. Small businesses in the construction industry must conduct regular risk assessments to ensure the safety of their workers and visitors to the site.

In addition to risk assessments, small businesses in the construction industry must also provide adequate training and supervision for their workers. This includes training on how to safely operate equipment, use personal protective equipment, and respond to emergencies. By ensuring that workers are properly trained, small businesses can reduce the risk of accidents and injuries on site.

Another important health and safety requirement for construction sites is the provision of first aid facilities and emergency response plans. Small businesses must have designated first aiders on site and ensure that they are trained to respond to emergencies effectively. In the event of an accident or injury, quick and effective first aid can make a significant difference in the outcome.

Overall, small business owners and managers in the construction industry must prioritize health and safety on their sites to protect their workers and avoid costly accidents. By following the necessary regulations, conducting regular risk assessments, providing adequate training, and implementing emergency response plans, small businesses can create a safe working environment for their employees.

Training Programs for Construction Workers

Training programs for construction workers are essential for ensuring the health and safety of employees in the construction industry. Small business owners and managers in the UK must prioritize providing comprehensive training to their construction workers to prevent accidents and injuries on the job site. These training programs cover a wide range of topics, including hazard recognition, proper tool and equipment usage, emergency response procedures, and personal protective equipment (PPE) requirements.

One key aspect of training programs for construction workers is hazard recognition. Workers must be able to identify potential hazards in their work environment to prevent accidents and injuries. By providing training on hazard recognition, small businesses can empower their employees to take proactive measures to mitigate risks and create a safer work environment. This training can include identifying common construction hazards such as falls, electrical hazards, and hazardous materials.

Proper tool and equipment usage training is also crucial for construction workers. Small business owners and managers in the UK must ensure that their employees are trained on how to safely operate tools and equipment to prevent accidents and injuries. This training can cover topics such as proper tool maintenance, correct usage techniques, and safety precautions to take when using specific tools and equipment. By providing comprehensive training in this area, small businesses can reduce the likelihood of workplace accidents and injuries.

Emergency response procedures training is another critical component of training programs for construction workers. Small business owners and managers in the UK must ensure that their employees are trained on how to respond to emergencies such as fires, chemical spills, and medical emergencies. This training can include developing emergency response plans, conducting regular drills, and providing employees with the necessary resources and tools to respond effectively in emergency situations. By preparing their employees through training, small businesses can minimize the impact of emergencies on their construction projects.

Lastly, training programs for construction workers should include education on personal protective equipment (PPE) requirements. Small business owners and managers in the UK must ensure that their employees are trained on how to properly use and maintain PPE to protect themselves from workplace hazards. This training can cover topics such as the different types of PPE available, when and how to use PPE, and the importance of wearing PPE at all times on the job site. By providing thorough training on PPE requirements, small businesses can ensure that their employees are adequately protected while working in the construction industry.

Creating a Culture of Safety in Construction Businesses

Creating a culture of safety in construction businesses is crucial for the well-being of employees and the success of the business. Small business owners and managers in the UK construction industry must prioritize health and safety to ensure a safe and productive work environment. By implementing proper safety protocols and training programs, businesses can reduce the risk of accidents and injuries on the job site.

One of the first steps in creating a culture of safety in construction businesses is to develop a comprehensive health and safety policy. This policy should outline the company's commitment to providing a safe workplace, as well as the specific procedures and protocols that employees must follow to ensure their own safety. By clearly communicating expectations and responsibilities, businesses can set the tone for a culture of safety within the organization.

In addition to having a health and safety policy, construction businesses should also invest in regular safety training for employees. This training should cover topics such as proper use of equipment, hazard identification, and emergency response procedures. By ensuring that employees are well-trained in safety protocols, businesses can reduce the likelihood of accidents and injuries on the job site.

Furthermore, small construction businesses in the UK should also conduct regular safety inspections and audits to identify potential hazards and ensure compliance with health and safety regulations. By proactively addressing safety issues, businesses can prevent accidents before they occur and create a safer work environment for employees.

In conclusion, creating a culture of safety in construction businesses is essential for protecting the well-being of employees and the success of the business. By developing a comprehensive health and safety policy, providing regular safety training, and conducting regular safety inspections, businesses can reduce the risk of accidents and injuries on the job site. Prioritizing health and safety not only benefits employees but also contributes to the overall success and sustainability of the business.

05

Chapter 5: Health and Safety Requirements for Food Service Establishments in the UK

Food Hygiene Regulations for Restaurants and Cafes

Food hygiene regulations for restaurants and cafes are crucial to ensure the health and safety of both employees and customers. In the UK, there are strict guidelines that must be followed to prevent foodborne illnesses and maintain a clean and sanitary environment. Small business owners and managers in the food service industry must be aware of these regulations and take the necessary steps to comply with them.

One of the key regulations for restaurants and cafes is the Food Safety Act 1990, which outlines the responsibilities of food business operators in ensuring that food is safe for consumption. This includes proper storage, preparation, and handling of food to prevent contamination. It is important for small business owners to have a thorough understanding of this act and implement food safety practices in their establishments.

In addition to the Food Safety Act, restaurants and cafes in the UK must also adhere to the Food Hygiene Regulations 2006. These regulations set out specific requirements for food hygiene, including the cleanliness of facilities, personal hygiene of staff, and proper maintenance of equipment. Small business owners should regularly review these regulations and make sure their staff are trained in food hygiene practices.

Another important aspect of food hygiene regulations for restaurants and cafes is the requirement for a Food Hygiene Certificate. This certificate demonstrates that the business has met certain hygiene standards and is compliant with regulations. Small business owners should ensure that their staff have the necessary training to obtain this certificate and display it prominently in their establishment.

Overall, food hygiene regulations for restaurants and cafes are essential for maintaining a safe and healthy environment for both employees and customers. Small business owners in the food service industry must stay informed about these regulations and take proactive measures to ensure compliance. By prioritizing food hygiene, businesses can protect their reputation, avoid fines, and most importantly, safeguard the health of their patrons.

Kitchen Safety Guidelines for Food Service Businesses

Kitchen safety is of utmost importance in any food service business, as it directly impacts the health and well-being of both employees and customers. As a small business owner or manager in the UK, it is crucial to establish and enforce kitchen safety guidelines to prevent accidents and ensure compliance with health and safety regulations. Here are some key guidelines to keep in mind:

First and foremost, all employees working in the kitchen should receive proper training on food safety and hygiene practices. This includes understanding proper food storage, handling, and cooking techniques to prevent foodborne illnesses. Regular training sessions should be conducted to reinforce these practices and keep employees up to date on any new regulations or guidelines.

Maintaining a clean and organized kitchen is essential to preventing accidents and maintaining a safe working environment. All surfaces should be regularly cleaned and sanitized, and any spills should be promptly cleaned up to prevent slips and falls. Additionally, all kitchen equipment should be properly maintained and inspected regularly to ensure it is safe to use.

Proper handling of sharp objects, such as knives and slicers, is crucial to prevent injuries in the kitchen. Employees should be trained on how to safely use and store these tools, as well as how to properly clean and maintain them. Safety guards should be in place on all equipment to prevent accidents, and employees should always use caution when handling sharp objects.

Fire safety is another important aspect of kitchen safety that should not be overlooked. All employees should be trained on how to properly use fire extinguishers and how to respond in the event of a fire. Additionally, regular fire drills should be conducted to ensure that everyone knows how to evacuate the kitchen safely in case of an emergency.

Lastly, it is important to have a first aid kit readily available in the kitchen in case of any injuries. Employees should be trained on basic first aid procedures, such as how to treat burns or cuts, and know when to seek medical attention. By following these kitchen safety guidelines, you can help ensure the health and well-being of everyone in your food service business.

Handling Food Allergies and Dietary Requirements

Handling food allergies and dietary requirements is an important aspect of running a successful small business in the UK, especially for those in the food service industry. It is crucial for small business owners and managers to be aware of the potential risks associated with food allergies and to have proper protocols in place to ensure the safety and well-being of their customers.

When it comes to food allergies, it is essential to educate your staff on the common allergies and the potential symptoms that may arise if a customer has an allergic reaction. Providing training on how to handle food safely and prevent cross-contamination is key to avoiding any incidents that could harm your customers.

In addition to allergies, dietary requirements such as vegetarian, vegan, gluten-free, and dairy-free options are becoming increasingly common. Small business owners should consider offering a variety of menu options to accommodate these dietary needs and clearly label any potential allergens in their dishes to inform customers.

It is also important to communicate openly with your customers about their dietary requirements and any allergies they may have. Providing a detailed menu that outlines all ingredients used in each dish can help customers make informed decisions about their food choices and prevent any potential allergic reactions.

By prioritizing the safety and well-being of your customers, you can build trust and loyalty within your business. Taking the necessary precautions to handle food allergies and dietary requirements not only protects your customers but also demonstrates your commitment to providing a safe and inclusive environment for all patrons. Remember, a little extra care and attention can go a long way in creating a positive dining experience for everyone.

06

Chapter 6: Health and Safety Protocols for Small Manufacturing Businesses in the UK

Safety Measures for Manufacturing Processes

Ensuring the safety of employees is a top priority for small manufacturing businesses in the UK. By implementing proper safety measures, business owners and managers can create a safe and healthy work environment for their employees. This not only reduces the risk of accidents and injuries but also boosts employee morale and productivity. In this subchapter, we will discuss some important safety measures that small manufacturing businesses can implement to ensure the well-being of their employees.

One of the most important safety measures for manufacturing processes is providing proper training to employees. Employees should be trained on how to operate machinery and equipment safely, as well as how to handle hazardous materials. Regular training sessions should be conducted to ensure that employees are up-to-date on safety protocols and procedures. By investing in training, small manufacturing businesses can prevent accidents and injuries in the workplace.

Another crucial safety measure for manufacturing processes is conducting regular safety inspections. Inspections should be carried out to identify any potential hazards or risks in the workplace. By addressing these issues promptly, business owners and managers can prevent accidents and injuries from occurring. Inspections should cover all aspects of the manufacturing process, from machinery and equipment to workspaces and storage areas.

In addition to training and inspections, small manufacturing businesses should also have proper safety protocols in place. This includes having emergency response plans for accidents or incidents that may occur in the workplace. Employees should be familiar with these protocols and know what to do in case of an emergency. By having clear safety protocols, businesses can minimize the impact of accidents and ensure the safety of their employees.

Furthermore, small manufacturing businesses should provide employees with the necessary personal protective equipment (PPE) to ensure their safety. This includes items such as goggles, gloves, helmets, and ear protection. Employees should be trained on how to properly use and maintain their PPE to maximize its effectiveness. By providing employees with the right PPE, businesses can prevent injuries and protect their workforce.

Overall, implementing these safety measures for manufacturing processes is essential for small businesses in the UK. By prioritizing the safety and well-being of employees, businesses can create a positive work environment and reduce the risk of accidents and injuries. By investing in training, inspections, safety protocols, and PPE, small manufacturing businesses can ensure the safety of their workforce and achieve long-term success.

Hazardous Material Handling in Manufacturing Environments

Hazardous material handling in manufacturing environments is a critical aspect of health and safety that small business owners and managers in the UK must pay close attention to. The improper handling of hazardous materials can have serious consequences, including harm to employees, damage to the environment, and legal repercussions. It is essential for businesses to have proper protocols in place to ensure the safe handling, storage, and disposal of hazardous materials.

One key aspect of hazardous material handling in manufacturing environments is the identification of hazardous substances. Businesses must be aware of the hazardous materials present in their workplace and ensure that employees are trained on how to safely handle these substances. This includes understanding the risks associated with each hazardous material, as well as how to properly store and transport them.

Another important consideration is the use of personal protective equipment (PPE) when handling hazardous materials. Employees should be provided with the appropriate PPE, such as gloves, goggles, and respirators, to protect themselves from exposure to harmful substances. It is the responsibility of employers to ensure that PPE is used correctly and that employees are trained on how to properly use and maintain their protective equipment.

Proper labeling of hazardous materials is also crucial in manufacturing environments. All hazardous materials should be clearly labeled with information such as the name of the substance, potential hazards, and safe handling instructions. This helps to ensure that employees are aware of the risks associated with each substance and can take the necessary precautions to protect themselves and others.

In conclusion, small business owners and managers in the UK must prioritize the safe handling of hazardous materials in manufacturing environments. By implementing proper protocols for identifying, handling, storing, and disposing of hazardous materials, businesses can protect their employees, the environment, and their bottom line. It is essential to stay informed about health and safety regulations related to hazardous material handling and to provide ongoing training to employees to ensure compliance and safety in the workplace.

Equipment Safety in Manufacturing Facilities

Equipment safety in manufacturing facilities is of utmost importance to ensure the well-being of employees and the smooth operation of the business. Small business owners and managers in the UK must adhere to strict health and safety regulations to prevent accidents and injuries in the workplace. Proper training and awareness of equipment safety protocols are essential for all employees working with machinery and tools in manufacturing facilities.

One of the key aspects of equipment safety in manufacturing facilities is regular maintenance and inspections of all machinery and equipment. Small business owners and managers must ensure that all equipment is in good working condition and that any defects or malfunctions are addressed promptly. Regular inspections can help identify potential hazards and prevent accidents before they occur.

Employees working with machinery and equipment in manufacturing facilities must also be properly trained on how to operate the equipment safely. Training sessions should cover proper operating procedures, safety precautions, and emergency response protocols. It is essential for small business owners and managers to invest in comprehensive training programs to ensure that all employees are equipped with the knowledge and skills necessary to work safely with equipment.

In addition to regular maintenance and training, small business owners and managers should also provide employees with personal protective equipment (PPE) to minimize the risk of injuries. PPE such as gloves, goggles, ear plugs, and safety helmets can help protect employees from hazards such as flying debris, loud noises, and chemical exposure. It is important for small business owners to ensure that employees wear PPE at all times when working with machinery and equipment.

Overall, equipment safety in manufacturing facilities is a critical aspect of maintaining a safe and healthy work environment. Small business owners and managers in the UK must prioritize equipment safety by implementing regular maintenance and inspections, providing comprehensive training to employees, and supplying necessary PPE. By following these guidelines, small businesses can reduce the risk of accidents and injuries in the workplace, ensuring the well-being of their employees and the success of their business.

Chapter 7: Occupational Health and Safety for Small Businesses in the UK

Employee Health and Well-being Programs

Employee Health and Well-being Programs are essential for small businesses in the UK to ensure the safety and well-being of their workforce. These programs not only promote a healthy work environment but also contribute to increased productivity and employee satisfaction. Small business owners and managers in the UK should consider implementing various initiatives to support the health and well-being of their employees.

One key aspect of Employee Health and Well-being Programs is promoting physical health through initiatives such as workplace wellness programs, gym memberships, and healthy eating options at the workplace. By encouraging employees to prioritize their physical health, small businesses can reduce absenteeism due to illness and improve overall employee well-being.

In addition to physical health, mental health and well-being initiatives are becoming increasingly important for small businesses in the UK. Providing access to mental health resources, such as counseling services or mental health awareness training, can help employees manage stress and improve their overall mental well-being. Small business owners and managers should prioritize mental health initiatives to create a supportive work environment for their employees.

Employee Health and Well-being Programs can also include initiatives to promote work-life balance, such as flexible working hours, remote work options, and paid time off for personal and family activities. By prioritizing work-life balance, small businesses can reduce burnout and improve employee retention rates.

Overall, implementing Employee Health and Well-being Programs is not only beneficial for the employees but also for the small business as a whole. By investing in the health and well-being of their workforce, small business owners and managers in the UK can create a positive work environment, improve employee satisfaction, and ultimately drive business success.

Preventing Work-Related Injuries and Illnesses

Preventing work-related injuries and illnesses is crucial for the success and well-being of small businesses in the UK. By implementing proper health and safety measures, small business owners and managers can create a safe and healthy work environment for their employees. This not only protects the workforce from harm but also helps to prevent costly lawsuits and downtime due to accidents or illnesses.

One of the key ways to prevent work-related injuries and illnesses is to conduct regular risk assessments. By identifying potential hazards in the workplace, such as slippery floors, faulty equipment, or poor lighting, small business owners can take steps to address these issues and prevent accidents from happening. It is important to involve employees in the risk assessment process, as they often have valuable insights into potential hazards that may not be immediately apparent.

Another important aspect of preventing work-related injuries and illnesses is providing adequate training for employees. This includes training on how to safely use equipment, proper lifting techniques, and emergency procedures. By ensuring that employees are well-trained and knowledgeable about health and safety protocols, small businesses can reduce the risk of accidents and injuries in the workplace.

In addition to training, small business owners should also establish clear health and safety policies and procedures. These guidelines should outline expectations for employees, as well as procedures for reporting hazards or injuries. By creating a culture of safety within the workplace, small businesses can help to prevent accidents and illnesses before they occur.

Overall, preventing work-related injuries and illnesses requires a proactive approach from small business owners and managers. By conducting risk assessments, providing training, and establishing clear policies, small businesses can create a safe and healthy work environment for their employees. By prioritizing health and safety, small businesses can protect their workforce and ensure the long-term success of their business.

Ergonomic Practices for Office and Retail Environments

In today's fast-paced business world, it is essential for small business owners and managers in the UK to prioritize the health and safety of their employees. One area that often gets overlooked is the importance of implementing ergonomic practices in office and retail environments. Ergonomics is the science of designing the workplace to fit the worker, rather than forcing the worker to fit the workplace. By incorporating ergonomic practices into your business operations, you can improve employee productivity, reduce the risk of injuries, and create a more comfortable working environment.

One key ergonomic practice for office and retail environments is ensuring that workstations are set up properly. This includes adjusting the height of desks and chairs to promote good posture, positioning computer monitors at eye level to reduce neck strain, and providing footrests for employees who sit for long periods of time. Additionally, it is important to encourage employees to take regular breaks to stretch and move around, as prolonged sitting can lead to musculoskeletal issues.

Another important aspect of ergonomic practices in office and retail environments is the design of the workspace itself. This includes ensuring that aisles are clear of obstructions to prevent trips and falls, installing anti-fatigue mats in areas where employees stand for long periods of time, and providing adequate lighting to reduce eye strain. By creating a well-designed workspace, you can help prevent accidents and injuries, as well as promote employee well-being and productivity.

In addition to physical ergonomics, it is also important to consider the mental and emotional well-being of employees in office and retail environments. This includes providing opportunities for stress relief, such as offering mindfulness or meditation sessions, creating a supportive work culture that encourages open communication and collaboration, and promoting work-life balance. By prioritizing the mental health of your employees, you can create a more positive and productive work environment.

Overall, incorporating ergonomic practices into your small business operations can have a significant impact on the health and safety of your employees. By focusing on proper workstation setup, workspace design, and mental well-being initiatives, you can create a safer, more comfortable, and more productive work environment for your employees. Remember, a healthy and happy workforce is key to the success of your business.

08

Chapter 8: Health and Safety Compliance for Small Businesses in the Hospitality Industry in the UK

Safety Regulations for Hotels, Bars, and Restaurants

Safety regulations for hotels, bars, and restaurants are crucial for ensuring the well-being of employees and customers alike. As a small business owner or manager in the UK, it is essential to be aware of and comply with these regulations to maintain a safe working environment. Failure to do so can result in serious consequences, including fines, lawsuits, and even closure of your establishment.

One important safety regulation to be aware of is the Health and Safety at Work Act 1974. This legislation requires employers to ensure the health, safety, and welfare of their employees, as well as anyone else who may be affected by their business activities. This includes implementing measures to prevent accidents, injuries, and illnesses in the workplace. As a small business owner or manager in the hospitality industry, it is your responsibility to familiarize yourself with this act and ensure that your business is compliant.

In addition to the Health and Safety at Work Act, there are specific regulations that apply to businesses in the hospitality industry, such as the Control of Substances Hazardous to Health (COSHH) Regulations 2002 and the Food Safety Act 1990. These regulations are designed to protect employees and customers from potential hazards, such as hazardous substances and contaminated food. By adhering to these regulations, you can create a safer environment for everyone who enters your establishment.

It is also important to provide adequate training for your employees on health and safety matters. This includes educating them on how to identify potential hazards, how to respond to emergencies, and how to use safety equipment properly. By investing in workplace safety training for your staff, you can reduce the risk of accidents and injuries in your establishment.

Overall, safety regulations for hotels, bars, and restaurants are essential for protecting the well-being of employees and customers. By staying informed about these regulations, providing necessary training for your staff, and maintaining a safe working environment, you can create a positive and secure atmosphere for everyone who visits your establishment. Remember, compliance with health and safety regulations is not just a legal requirement – it is also a moral obligation to ensure the welfare of those in your care.

Staff Training for Health and Safety in Hospitality Businesses

Staff training for health and safety in hospitality businesses is crucial to ensure the well-being of employees and customers alike. In the fast-paced and dynamic environment of the hospitality industry, it is essential for small business owners and managers in the UK to invest in comprehensive training programs to mitigate risks and comply with health and safety regulations.

One of the key aspects of staff training for health and safety in hospitality businesses is ensuring that employees are aware of potential hazards in the workplace. From slippery floors to hot surfaces in the kitchen, employees must be trained to identify and address these risks to prevent accidents and injuries. Regular training sessions should cover topics such as proper lifting techniques, fire safety protocols, and emergency response procedures to equip staff with the knowledge and skills needed to handle any situation that may arise.

In addition to hazard awareness, staff training for health and safety in hospitality businesses should also focus on promoting a culture of safety within the organization. This includes fostering open communication channels for reporting potential hazards, encouraging employees to take ownership of their own safety, and recognizing and rewarding safe behaviors. By instilling a culture of safety, small businesses in the UK can create a positive work environment where employees feel valued and supported in their efforts to maintain a safe workplace. Furthermore, staff training for health and safety in hospitality businesses should also address the specific health and safety regulations that apply to the industry. From food handling and hygiene standards to noise and vibration exposure limits, employees must be aware of the legal requirements that govern their work environment. Regular training sessions should cover updates to regulations and guidelines to ensure that staff are always up-to-date with the latest requirements.

Overall, investing in staff training for health and safety in hospitality businesses is an essential step towards creating a safe and healthy work environment. By providing employees with the knowledge, skills, and resources they need to stay safe on the job, small business owners and managers in the UK can protect their workforce, reduce the risk of accidents and injuries, and demonstrate their commitment to maintaining high standards of health and safety in the hospitality industry.

Managing Health and Safety Risks in Guest Services

Managing health and safety risks in guest services is essential for small businesses in the UK to ensure the well-being of both employees and customers. By implementing proper protocols and guidelines, businesses can create a safe environment for everyone involved. This subchapter will explore key strategies for managing health and safety risks in guest services, with a focus on small businesses in the UK.

One of the first steps in managing health and safety risks in guest services is conducting a thorough risk assessment. This involves identifying potential hazards in the workplace, such as slippery floors or faulty equipment, and taking steps to mitigate these risks. By regularly reviewing and updating risk assessments, businesses can ensure that they are proactively addressing potential safety concerns.

Training plays a crucial role in managing health and safety risks in guest services. All employees should receive comprehensive training on relevant health and safety protocols, including proper lifting techniques, emergency procedures, and hygiene practices. By investing in ongoing training for employees, businesses can help prevent accidents and injuries in the workplace.

In addition to training, small businesses in the UK should also have clear health and safety policies in place for guest services. These policies should outline expectations for employees, as well as procedures for reporting incidents or concerns. By communicating these policies effectively to all staff members, businesses can promote a culture of safety and accountability in the workplace.

Regular monitoring and review of health and safety practices are essential for small businesses in the UK. By regularly assessing the effectiveness of their health and safety protocols, businesses can identify areas for improvement and make necessary adjustments. By staying proactive and diligent in managing health and safety risks in guest services, businesses can create a safe and welcoming environment for employees and customers alike.

Chapter 9: Mental Health and Well-being Initiatives for Small Businesses in the UK

Promoting Mental Health Awareness in the Workplace

Promoting Mental Health Awareness in the Workplace is essential for small business owners and managers in the UK. Mental health issues can have a significant impact on employee well-being, productivity, and overall company performance. By raising awareness and implementing strategies to support mental health in the workplace, small businesses can create a positive and supportive work environment for their employees.

One way to promote mental health awareness in the workplace is to provide training and education for employees and managers. This can include workshops on stress management, mental health first aid, and how to recognize the signs of mental health issues in the workplace. By increasing awareness and understanding of mental health, employees and managers can better support each other and create a more inclusive and supportive work environment.

In addition to training and education, small businesses can also implement policies and procedures to support mental health in the workplace. This can include flexible working arrangements, access to mental health resources and support services, and promoting a culture of open communication and support. By creating a supportive and inclusive workplace culture, small businesses can help reduce stigma around mental health and encourage employees to seek help when needed.

Small business owners and managers in the UK should also consider implementing mental health and well-being initiatives in the workplace. This can include wellness programs, employee assistance programs, and mental health awareness campaigns. By prioritizing mental health and well-being in the workplace, small businesses can create a positive and supportive work environment that benefits both employees and the company as a whole.

Overall, promoting mental health awareness in the workplace is crucial for small businesses in the UK. By providing training, implementing policies and procedures, and offering support and resources, small businesses can create a supportive and inclusive work environment that prioritizes employee well-being. By taking steps to support mental health in the workplace, small businesses can help improve employee morale, productivity, and overall company performance.

Providing Support for Employees' Mental Health Needs

As small business owners and managers in the UK, it is crucial to recognize and address the mental health needs of your employees. The well-being of your workforce directly impacts productivity, morale, and overall success of your business. By prioritizing mental health support, you can create a positive work environment where employees feel valued and supported. One way to provide support for employees' mental health needs is to offer access to resources and services such as Employee Assistance Programs (EAPs) or mental health hotlines. These services can provide confidential counseling and support to employees who may be struggling with stress, anxiety, depression, or other mental health issues. By offering these resources, you are showing your employees that their well-being is a top priority.

In addition to external resources, it is important to create a work culture that promotes open communication and destigmatizes mental health discussions. Encouraging employees to talk openly about their feelings and struggles can help create a supportive and understanding environment. Consider implementing mental health awareness training for managers and supervisors to equip them with the skills to recognize signs of distress and provide appropriate support.

Flexible work arrangements can also be beneficial in supporting employees' mental health needs. Allowing for remote work options, flexible hours, or mental health days can help employees better manage their work-life balance and reduce stress. By accommodating individual needs and promoting a healthy work-life balance, you are fostering a more positive and productive work environment. Overall, providing support for employees' mental health needs is not only beneficial for your workforce but also for the success of your business. By prioritizing mental health, you can create a more engaged, productive, and loyal team. Remember, a mentally healthy workforce is a key ingredient to a successful and thriving business.

Creating a Healthy Work Environment for Mental Well-being

Creating a healthy work environment for mental well-being is crucial for the overall success and productivity of small businesses in the UK. As a small business owner or manager, it is important to prioritize the mental health and well-being of your employees. By fostering a positive work environment, you can help reduce stress, improve morale, and increase employee satisfaction.

One way to create a healthy work environment for mental well-being is by promoting open communication and transparency within your organization. Encourage employees to express their thoughts and concerns, and be receptive to feedback. By fostering a culture of open communication, you can help build trust and create a supportive work environment.

Another key aspect of promoting mental well-being in the workplace is by providing resources and support for employees. This can include offering employee assistance programs, mental health training, and access to counseling services. By providing these resources, you can help employees manage their stress, anxiety, and other mental health issues effectively.

In addition to providing resources and support, it is important to encourage work-life balance among your employees. Encourage them to take breaks, use their vacation time, and prioritize self-care. By promoting work-life balance, you can help prevent burnout and improve overall mental well-being in the workplace.

Overall, creating a healthy work environment for mental well-being requires a proactive approach from small business owners and managers. By promoting open communication, providing resources and support, and encouraging work-life balance, you can help foster a positive work environment that supports the mental health and well-being of your employees. By prioritizing mental well-being in the workplace, you can create a more productive and successful business.

10

Chapter 10: Health and Safety Considerations for Small Businesses Operating Remotely in the UK

Remote Work Safety Guidelines

Remote work has become increasingly common in today's business landscape, offering flexibility and convenience for both employees and employers. However, it is important for small business owners and managers to ensure that their remote workers are following safety guidelines to prevent accidents and injuries. In this subchapter, we will outline some key safety guidelines for remote work to help keep your employees safe and healthy.

First and foremost, it is important for remote workers to have a designated workspace that is free from hazards. This includes ensuring that the area is well-lit, comfortable, and ergonomically designed to prevent strain and injury. Additionally, remote workers should have access to necessary equipment, such as a computer, phone, and any other tools needed to perform their job effectively.

Another important safety guideline for remote work is to establish clear communication channels between employees and managers. This includes setting regular check-ins, providing access to support and resources, and ensuring that all employees are aware of emergency procedures. By maintaining open lines of communication, managers can help remote workers feel supported and connected to the rest of the team.

Additionally, small business owners and managers should provide training on health and safety protocols specific to remote work. This may include information on how to set up a safe workspace, how to prevent musculoskeletal injuries, and how to maintain good mental health while working remotely. By educating employees on these topics, businesses can help prevent accidents and injuries before they occur.

Finally, it is important for small business owners and managers to regularly assess and review their remote work safety guidelines. As technology and work practices evolve, it is essential to stay up-to-date on best practices and make any necessary adjustments to ensure the health and safety of remote workers. By prioritizing safety and well-being, small businesses can create a positive and productive work environment for their remote employees.

Cybersecurity Measures for Remote Workers

In today's digital age, remote work has become increasingly common among small businesses in the UK. With the rise of remote work comes the need for enhanced cybersecurity measures to protect sensitive data and information. Small business owners and managers must prioritize cybersecurity to ensure the safety and security of their remote workers. This subchapter will explore some essential cybersecurity measures that small businesses can implement to protect their remote workers.

One crucial cybersecurity measure for remote workers is the use of secure and encrypted communication channels. Small businesses should encourage their remote workers to use encrypted messaging apps and virtual private networks (VPNs) to communicate securely. By using these tools, remote workers can protect their communications from potential cyber threats and hackers.

Another important cybersecurity measure for remote workers is the use of strong and unique passwords. Small businesses should educate their remote workers on the importance of using complex passwords that are difficult to guess. Additionally, remote workers should be encouraged to use two-factor authentication for an extra layer of security.

Regular software updates and patches are also essential for maintaining cybersecurity for remote workers. Small businesses should ensure that all devices used by remote workers are up to date with the latest software updates and security patches. By keeping their devices updated, remote workers can protect themselves from vulnerabilities that could be exploited by cybercriminals.

Small businesses should also implement remote access controls to limit the access of remote workers to sensitive data and information. By restricting access based on job roles and responsibilities, small businesses can reduce the risk of data breaches and unauthorized access. Remote workers should only have access to the information and resources necessary to perform their job duties.

Lastly, small businesses should provide cybersecurity training and awareness programs for their remote workers. By educating remote workers on best practices for cybersecurity, small businesses can empower their employees to recognize and respond to potential threats. Training programs should cover topics such as phishing scams, social engineering attacks, and data protection practices. By investing in cybersecurity training, small businesses can create a culture of security awareness among their remote workforce.

Communication and Emergency Response Plans for Remote Teams

Communication is key when it comes to ensuring the health and safety of remote teams in small businesses. Having a well-thought-out emergency response plan in place is crucial for addressing any unforeseen situations that may arise. This subchapter will delve into the importance of effective communication and emergency response plans for remote teams in the UK.

In order to effectively communicate with remote teams, it is essential to establish clear channels of communication. Whether it be through email, phone calls, video conferencing, or messaging apps, having reliable methods of communication in place is vital for keeping remote teams informed and connected. Regular check-ins and updates can help to ensure that everyone is on the same page and aware of any potential risks or emergencies.

When it comes to emergency response planning for remote teams, it is important to consider the unique challenges that come with working remotely. Ensuring that all team members are aware of the emergency procedures and protocols is crucial for a swift and effective response in the event of an emergency. Regular training and drills can help to familiarize remote workers with what to do in different emergency scenarios.

Small business owners and managers in the UK should also consider the specific needs and circumstances of their remote teams when developing emergency response plans. Factors such as the nature of the work being done, the location of team members, and any potential hazards should all be taken into account when creating a comprehensive emergency response plan. It is important to tailor the plan to fit the specific needs of the remote team.

By prioritizing effective communication and emergency response planning, small businesses in the UK can ensure the health and safety of their remote teams. Proactive measures such as regular communication, training, and drills can help to mitigate risks and ensure that remote workers are prepared for any potential emergencies. Taking the time to develop a thorough emergency response plan can make all the difference in ensuring the well-being of remote teams in small businesses.

Chapter 11: First Aid and Emergency Response Planning for Small Businesses in the UK

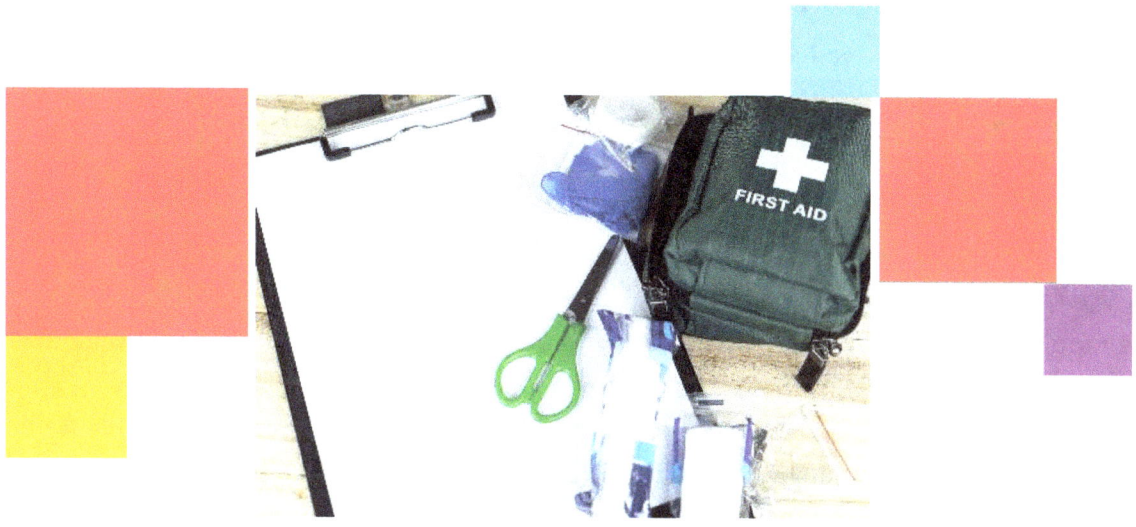

Establishing First Aid Protocols in the Workplace

In any workplace, accidents and injuries can happen unexpectedly. That's why it is crucial for small business owners and managers in the UK to establish first aid protocols in their workplaces. Having clear procedures in place can help ensure the safety and well-being of employees in case of an emergency.

First and foremost, small businesses should designate one or more employees to be trained in first aid. These individuals should undergo proper training and certification to handle various medical emergencies that may arise in the workplace. It is important to have these trained individuals readily available during working hours to provide immediate assistance when needed.

Furthermore, small businesses should ensure that first aid kits are readily available and fully stocked at all times. These kits should include essential items such as bandages, gauze, antiseptic wipes, and gloves. Regular checks should be conducted to ensure that all items are in good condition and within their expiration dates.

In addition to having trained first aiders and well-equipped first aid kits, small businesses should also establish clear procedures for reporting and responding to injuries or emergencies. Employees should be informed about who to contact in case of an emergency and what steps to take to provide assistance until professional help arrives.

By establishing first aid protocols in the workplace, small business owners and managers in the UK can create a safe and secure environment for their employees. Investing in proper training, equipment, and procedures can make a significant difference in ensuring the health and well-being of everyone in the workplace. Remember, being prepared is key to effectively managing emergencies and preventing further harm.

Emergency Response Plans for Different Scenarios

Creating an emergency response plan is essential for small businesses in the UK, regardless of their industry. In the event of unforeseen circumstances such as fires, accidents, or medical emergencies, having a well-thought-out plan in place can save lives and prevent further damage. Different scenarios require different approaches, so it is important for small business owners and managers to tailor their emergency response plans accordingly.

For retail businesses in the UK, it is crucial to have a clear evacuation plan in case of a fire or other emergency that requires employees and customers to leave the premises quickly and safely. This plan should outline designated escape routes, assembly points, and procedures for accounting for all individuals. Regular drills and training sessions should be conducted to ensure that everyone knows what to do in the event of an emergency.

In small medical practices, the focus of the emergency response plan should be on providing immediate medical assistance to patients and staff. This may involve having first aid kits readily available, designating individuals to be trained in CPR and basic life support, and establishing communication protocols with emergency services. It is also important to have contingency plans for power outages or other disruptions that could affect patient care.

For small construction businesses in the UK, the emergency response plan should address the unique risks associated with working on construction sites. This may include procedures for dealing with accidents involving heavy machinery, falls from heights, or hazardous materials. It is essential to have a clear chain of command and communication system in place to ensure that emergencies are responded to quickly and effectively.

In food service establishments, the emergency response plan should focus on preventing foodborne illnesses and ensuring the safety of both employees and customers. This may involve implementing hygiene protocols, training employees in safe food handling practices, and having procedures in place for dealing with food contamination incidents. Regular inspections and audits can help to identify potential risks and ensure compliance with health and safety regulations.

In the manufacturing sector, the emergency response plan should address the specific hazards associated with operating machinery, handling chemicals, and working in confined spaces. This may include providing personal protective equipment, conducting regular safety inspections, and training employees in emergency response procedures. It is important to have contingency plans for potential equipment malfunctions, chemical spills, or other emergencies that could threaten the health and safety of workers.

Training Employees in First Aid and Emergency Procedures

Training employees in first aid and emergency procedures is a crucial aspect of ensuring the health and safety of your workforce. In the event of an emergency, having well-trained employees who can respond quickly and effectively can make all the difference. This subchapter will outline the importance of training employees in first aid and emergency procedures, as well as provide practical tips for implementing such training in your small business.

First and foremost, training employees in first aid and emergency procedures can save lives. In the event of a medical emergency or accident, having employees who are trained in first aid can mean the difference between life and death. By equipping your employees with the knowledge and skills to respond effectively in emergencies, you are not only protecting the health and safety of your workforce, but also demonstrating your commitment to their well-being.

In addition to potentially saving lives, training employees in first aid and emergency procedures can also help to prevent further injuries or damage in the event of an emergency. By having employees who are trained to respond quickly and appropriately to emergencies, you can minimize the impact of accidents and injuries in the workplace. This can ultimately reduce the likelihood of costly legal claims and insurance payouts, as well as improve the overall safety culture within your small business.

When it comes to implementing first aid and emergency procedure training in your small business, it is important to tailor the training to the specific needs and risks of your workplace. Consider conducting a risk assessment to identify potential hazards and determine the appropriate level of training required for your employees. This may include basic first aid training, CPR certification, and specific emergency response procedures for different types of incidents.

Furthermore, it is important to regularly review and update your first aid and emergency procedures training to ensure that employees are up-to-date on the latest protocols and best practices. Consider scheduling refresher training sessions on a regular basis, as well as incorporating emergency drills and simulations into your training program. By investing in the ongoing training and development of your employees, you can ensure that they are well-prepared to respond effectively in the event of an emergency.

Small Business Health and Safety: A Guide for UK Businesses

Small Business Health and Safety: A Guide for UK Businesses

12

Conclusion: Ensuring a Safe and Healthy Work Environment for Small Businesses in the UK

In conclusion, it is imperative for small businesses in the UK to prioritize the health and safety of their employees in order to create a safe and productive work environment. By implementing proper health and safety measures, businesses can prevent accidents and injuries, reduce absenteeism, and improve overall employee well-being. This not only benefits the employees themselves, but also the business as a whole by increasing efficiency and reducing costs associated with workplace accidents.

One of the key ways to ensure a safe and healthy work environment for small businesses in the UK is to stay informed about health and safety regulations specific to their industry. Whether it be retail, medical, construction, food service, manufacturing, hospitality, or any other niche, understanding and complying with industry-specific regulations is essential for maintaining a safe workplace. By staying up-to-date on regulations and guidelines, businesses can proactively address potential hazards and risks before they become serious issues.

Additionally, providing workplace safety training to employees is crucial for ensuring their well-being. Small businesses in the UK should invest in training programs that educate employees on how to identify and mitigate risks, operate machinery safely, and respond to emergencies. By empowering employees with the knowledge and skills to prioritize safety, businesses can create a culture of safety and reduce the likelihood of workplace accidents.

Furthermore, small businesses in the UK should develop and implement health and safety protocols tailored to their specific operations. This may include conducting regular risk assessments, implementing safety procedures for hazardous tasks, and establishing emergency response plans. By customizing health and safety protocols to fit the unique needs of the business, owners and managers can effectively protect their employees and minimize the potential for accidents or injuries.

In conclusion, small businesses in the UK must prioritize the health and safety of their employees in order to create a safe and healthy work environment. By staying informed about industry-specific regulations, providing workplace safety training, developing customized health and safety protocols, and fostering a culture of safety, businesses can protect their employees and ensure their well-being. Ultimately, investing in health and safety measures is not only a legal requirement, but also a smart business decision that can lead to increased productivity, reduced costs, and a positive work environment for all.

Small Business Health and Safety - A guide for UK Businesses

Tim Wiskin is a Chartered Safety Professional and registered Consultant with the UK OSHCR register. Tim has spent the last 30 years working in Health and Safety in some form and as a Health and Safety Manager and Consultant for the last 22 years, having worked in the aviation, manufacturing, chemical industries and in consultancy. Tim is the Managing Director and principle consultant of Norcam Ltd and is also an volunteer Community First Responder for an NHS Ambulance Service.

Norcam Ltd provide Health, Safety and Environment consultancy services along with training in a wide variety of Health & Safety, First Aid and Mental Health subjects.

Tim can be reached at tim.wiskin@norcamltd.com and through www.norcamltd.com

www.ingramcontent.com/pod-product-compliance
Lightning Source LLC
Chambersburg PA
CBHW062316220526
45479CB00004B/1185